Summer Handwriting hots up with CGP!

It's crucial to keep working on Handwriting skills throughout Year 3, and this CGP book is a brilliant way to keep pupils practising regularly...

It's packed with fun, engaging exercises for every day of summer term, covering all the words they'll need to use most often.

We've included plenty of full sentences and longer pieces to tackle too — perfect for helping them build up their fluency and confidence!

What CGP is all about

Our sole aim here at CGP is to produce the highest quality books — carefully written, immaculately presented and dangerously close to being funny.

Then we work our socks off to get them out to you — at the cheapest possible prices.

Contents

☑ Use the tick boxes to help keep a record of which pages have been attempted.

Week 1
- ☑ Day 1 1
- ☑ Day 2 2
- ☑ Day 3 3
- ☑ Day 4 4
- ☑ Day 5 5

Week 2
- ☑ Day 1 6
- ☑ Day 2 7
- ☑ Day 3 8
- ☑ Day 4 9
- ☑ Day 5 10

Week 3
- ☑ Day 1 11
- ☑ Day 2 12
- ☑ Day 3 13
- ☑ Day 4 14
- ☑ Day 5 15

Week 4
- ☑ Day 1 16
- ☑ Day 2 17
- ☑ Day 3 18
- ☑ Day 4 19
- ☑ Day 5 20

Week 5
- ☑ Day 1 21
- ☑ Day 2 22
- ☑ Day 3 23
- ☑ Day 4 24
- ☑ Day 5 25

Week 6
- ☑ Day 1 26
- ☑ Day 2 27
- ☑ Day 3 28
- ☑ Day 4 29
- ☑ Day 5 30

Week 7
- ☑ Day 1 31
- ☑ Day 2 32
- ☑ Day 3 33
- ☑ Day 4 34
- ☑ Day 5 35

Week 8
- ☑ Day 1 36
- ☑ Day 2 37
- ☑ Day 3 38
- ☑ Day 4 39
- ☑ Day 5 40

Week 9

- [✓] Day 1 41
- [✓] Day 2 42
- [✓] Day 3 43
- [✓] Day 4 44
- [✓] Day 5 45

Week 10

- [✓] Day 1 46
- [✓] Day 2 47
- [✓] Day 3 48
- [✓] Day 4 49
- [✓] Day 5 50

Week 11

- [✓] Day 1 51
- [✓] Day 2 52
- [✓] Day 3 53
- [✓] Day 4 54
- [✓] Day 5 55

Week 12

- [✓] Day 1 56
- [✓] Day 2 57
- [✓] Day 3 58
- [✓] Day 4 59
- [✓] Day 5 60

Published by CGP

ISBN: 978 1 78908 663 8

Editors: Luke Bennett, Ellen Burton, Eleanor Crabtree and Hayley Thompson.

With thanks to Sharon Keeley-Holden and Lucy Towle for the proofreading.
With thanks to Emily Smith for the copyright research.

Printed by Elanders Ltd, Newcastle upon Tyne.
Clipart on the cover and throughout the book from Corel®
Based on the classic CGP style created by Richard Parsons.

Text, design, layout and original illustrations © Coordination Group Publications Ltd. (CGP) 2020
All rights reserved.

Photocopying this book is not permitted, even if you have a CLA licence.
Extra copies are available from CGP with next day delivery • 0800 1712 712 • www.cgpbooks.co.uk

How to Use this Book

- This book contains 60 pages of daily handwriting practice.

- It's split into 12 sections — that's roughly one section for each week of the Year 3 Summer term.

- A week is made up of 5 pages, so there's one for every school day of the term (Monday – Friday).

- Each page should take about 10 minutes to complete.

- Each week, pupils practise copying individual words, such as spelling words from the National Curriculum, then whole sentences and paragraphs with a particular theme. This helps them to build up their handwriting fluency.

- A typical page looks something like this:

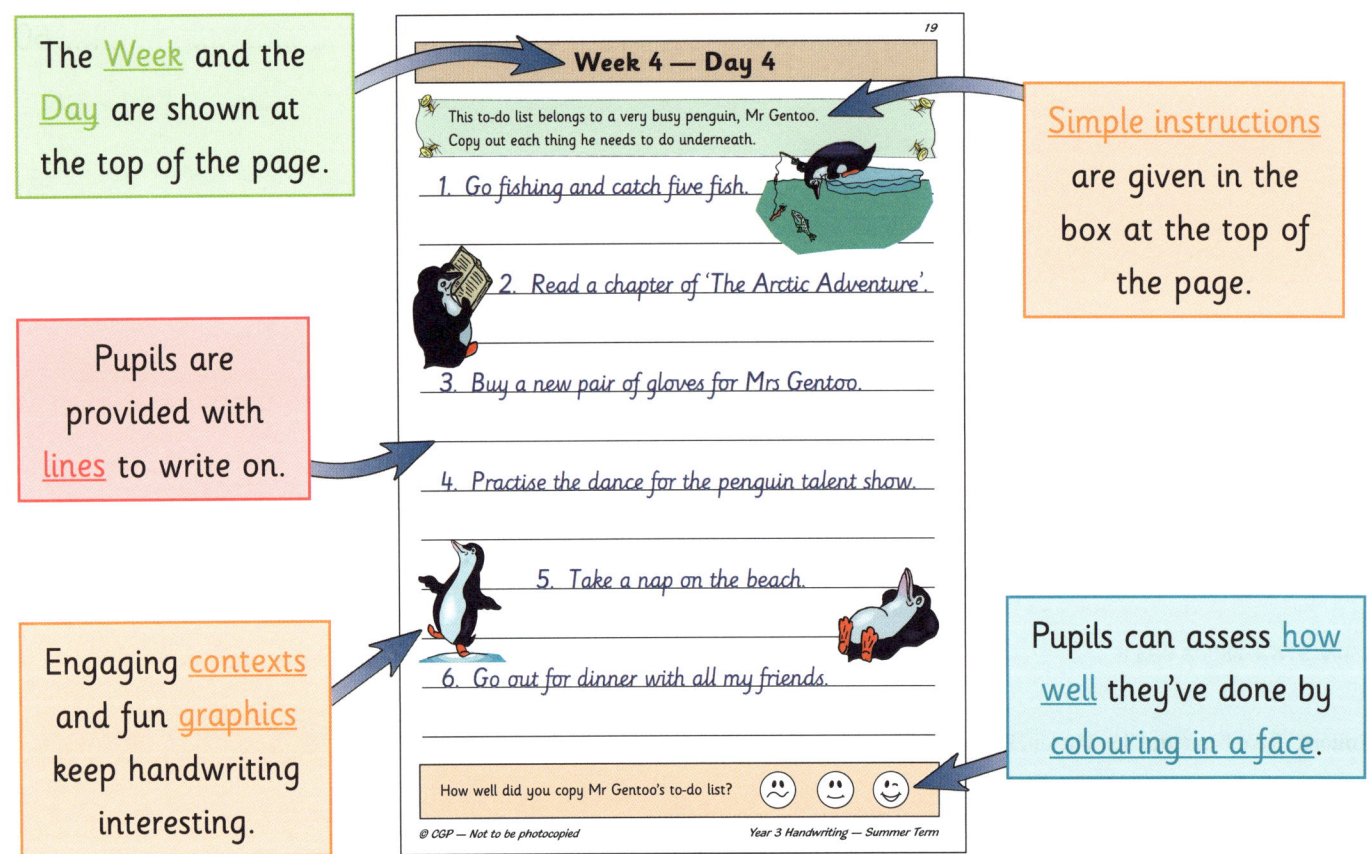

The Week and the Day are shown at the top of the page.

Simple instructions are given in the box at the top of the page.

Pupils are provided with lines to write on.

Engaging contexts and fun graphics keep handwriting interesting.

Pupils can assess how well they've done by colouring in a face.

If you are a parent or guardian using this book at home with your child, you should bear in mind that different schools have different handwriting styles. You should check with the school to see how they write and join each letter. Some schools also have different break letters (letters that don't join to the next letter). For example, 'g' can be a break letter or can be joined. You should check which break letters the school uses.

Week 1 — Day 1

Each of these words has a pair of vowels in it.
Copy each word out three times.

tourist

teacher

question

mermaid

height

fifteen

poetry

cookery

toaster

tortoise

sausage

shield

How did you get on with these words?

Week 1 — Day 2

Each of these words has at least one pair of consonants in it. Copy each word out three times.

thunder

throne

history

flower

golden

walking

festival

basket

problem

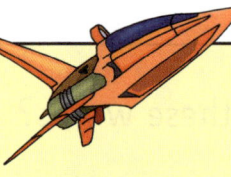

spaceship

broken

mustard

How do you think this page went?

Week 1 — Day 3

Here are twelve words containing double letters. Copy each one out three times. Write as neatly as you can.

coffee

puzzled

mammals

hammock

zookeeper

balloon

tennis

sitting

warrior

bubbles

unhappy

address

How did you find this page?

Week 1 — Day 4

Each of these sentences contains at least one word with double letters. Copy each of these sentences out below.

My whole basket of eggs got broken.

Fifteen balloons were not enough to help him fly.

The unhappy mermaid was jealous of the tourists.

Our teacher drinks lots of strong coffee.

The puzzled queen is sitting on her throne.

The zookeeper read poetry to the old tortoise.

How neatly did you write these sentences?

Week 1 — Day 5

This poem contains lots of alliteration. Alliteration is when the same sound is repeated at the start of words. Copy out the poem below.

At the pet shop down the street,

the furry ferrets ran round my feet,

the cute cats curled up on my knees,

the dirty dogs were full of fleas,

the happy hamster hoped for a treat,

and the colourful canary said, "tweet tweet".

How did you get on with this poem?

Week 2 — Day 1

The words on this page all end in 'ous'. Copy out each one twice.

jealous

curious

furious

mischievous

famous

glamorous

enormous

disastrous

dangerous

mountainous

courageous

adventurous

How did you get on with these words?

Week 2 — Day 2

Copy out these sentences. They all contain a word ending in 'ous'.

The potion was a poisonous green colour.

Shanice loved riding her fabulous new bike.

Everyone said the party was a tremendous success.

Kamil was serious about winning the trophy.

Grandpa Joe has various hobbies.

It is courteous to hold the door open for someone.

How did you get on with these sentences?

Week 2 — Day 3

Copy out each of these sentences as neatly as you can.

"My heart is broken!" sobbed Sylvia loudly.

Pineapples are my second favourite fruit.

This isn't a sentence I thought I'd ever have to write.

 The king's reign was the longest in history.

"Perhaps you could occasionally tidy up," said Dad.

Marvin had a peculiar exercise routine.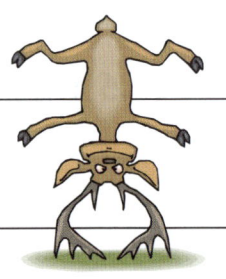

How are your sentences looking?

Week 2 — Day 4

Here is the beginning of a mysterious story. Copy out each line below.

It was a dark, stormy night in Little Hamling.

The rain lashed down as the wind whipped the trees

overhead. As the clock struck twelve, two figures

appeared at the end of the lane. "Ssh," said one.

"We'll be safe here until the morning.

They don't know we've escaped yet..."

Does this page look nice and neat?

Week 2 — Day 5

Copy out this description of a dangerous journey on the lines below.

The group came to a halt at the edge of the cliff. Far below, the river tumbled and roared over the treacherous rocks. There was a narrow, wooden bridge ahead, its planks slimy and rotten with age. A thick mist made it difficult to see. "I think it's this way," gulped Cherie.

Was your handwriting dangerously good here?

Week 3 — Day 1

All the words on this page end with 'tion'. Copy each word out twice.

action

auction

station

potion

correction

ambition

invention

migration

construction

competition

information

fascination

How are your 'tion' words looking?

Week 3 — Day 2

 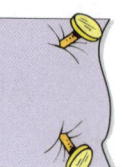

These sentences all contain words ending in 'tion'.
Neatly copy each sentence out onto the line below.

Hedgehogs go into hibernation in winter.

_____

"Did I mention our pet cat?" said Cleo.

_____

My favourite type of book to read is science fiction.

_____

 The race seemed to happen in slow motion.

_____

Zahara helped herself to a large portion of lasagne.

_____

My teacher says I have a vivid imagination.

_____

How did you get on with these sentences?

Week 3 — Day 3

Copy out the sentences below in your best handwriting.

Class 3A will have a grammar test on Monday.

Everybody at the party shouted, "Surprise!"

Errol the dog could be quite naughty.

Alice was certain they'd gone in a complete circle.

"Stop! I've heard enough," roared the king.

Luckily, I have two magic potatoes in my possession.

Do your sentences look smashing today?

Week 3 — Day 4

The list below was written by an inventor. Copy out each line. Which invention would you most like to have?

Here is a list of my best ideas:

1. A car that runs on banana peels and popcorn.

2. A robot that cleans out your hamster's cage.

3. A rollercoaster that takes you to school.

4. My own personal pair of wings.

5. Shoes that let you walk on water.

How is your list looking?

Week 3 — Day 5

Here is an advert for a really useful robot. Copy it out in the space below.

Need some help around the house?

Not enough hours in the day?

Then Robo-4000 is the robot for you! Robo-4000 dusts, tidies and cleans the toilet without complaint. You don't even need to feed him! Comes in a choice of three colours. Absolutely no refunds.

How neat is your advert?

Week 4 — Day 1

Here are twelve words that end in 'sion'.
Copy each word out twice.

tension

mission

revision

occasion

profession

television

obsession

decision

percussion

expansion

explosion

precision

How neatly did you write these words?

Week 4 — Day 2

There are six sentences on this page. Each sentence contains one or more words that end in 'sion'. Copy the sentences out underneath.

I asked Dad for permission to buy some sweets.

Last night, I dreamt there was an alien invasion.

Thea has an obsession with purple flowers.

Our teachers are having a discussion.

They are building an extension for their mansion.

There was a collision between the cat and the duck.

How did you find these sentences?

Week 4 — Day 3

Copy each of these sentences out underneath.
Write each word as neatly as you can.

"Sorry, it was an accident," said the naughty girl.

Owen is supposed to take his medicine every day.

Please remember to do your history homework.

Alisha is the most famous parrot of all.

One quarter of the books in my library are invisible.

Noah's birthday is on the eighth of February.

How is your writing looking?

Week 4 — Day 4

This to-do list belongs to a very busy penguin, Mr Gentoo. Copy out each thing he needs to do underneath.

1. Go fishing and catch five fish.

2. Read a chapter of 'The Arctic Adventure'.

3. Buy a new pair of gloves for Mrs Gentoo.

4. Practise the dance for the penguin talent show.

5. Take a nap on the beach.

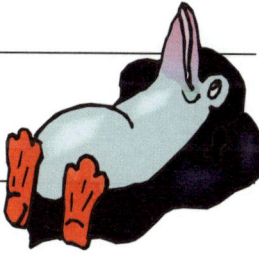

6. Go out for dinner with all my friends.

How well did you copy Mr Gentoo's to-do list?

Week 4 — Day 5

Sakiya has lost her pet unicorn. She put this notice up around the town. Copy it out below.

Missing unicorn. Have you seen this unicorn? It was last seen on Monday evening in the park. It has a long horn and a bright golden mane. You will be granted one wish as a reward for finding it. If you have any information, please contact Sakiya.

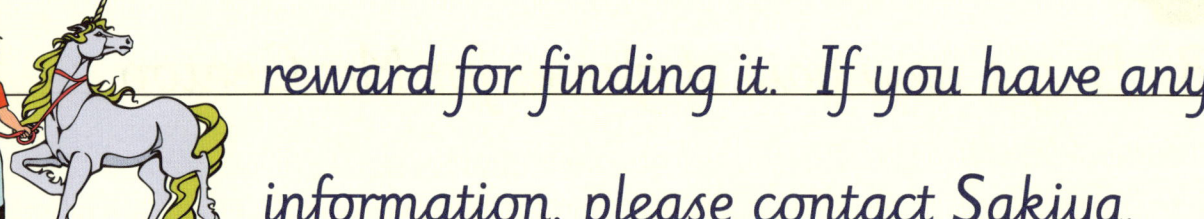

How did this page go?

Week 5 — Day 1

These words all end in 'cian'. Copy each one out twice.

musician

physician

magician

politician

optician

statistician

electrician

technician

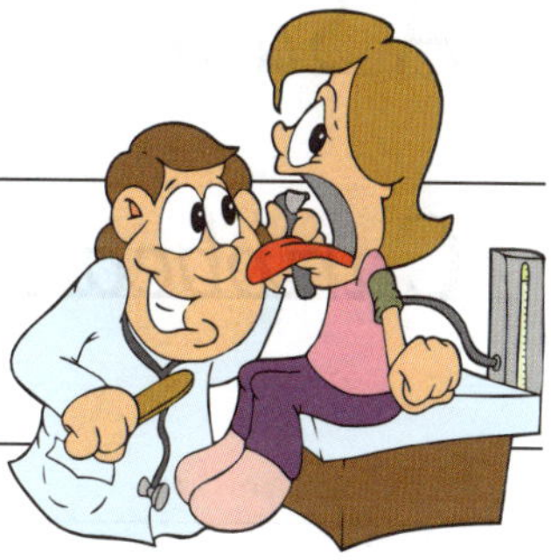

dietician

paediatrician

How neat are your words looking?

Week 5 — Day 2

These sentences all contain a word ending in 'cian'.
Copy each sentence out neatly underneath.

The beautician put make-up on the bride.

"I want to be a politician," said Rani.

Do not touch this priceless Grecian vase.

You need to be a good mathematician for this job.

A Saint Lucian is a person from the Caribbean island of Saint Lucia.

How do your sentences look?

Week 5 — Day 3

Copy each of these sentences out as neatly as you can.

The tour guide couldn't answer the question.

They sat at opposite ends of the dinner table.

"This isn't my regular haircut!" cried Tony.

Meet me at the library at quarter past two.

What is the purpose of this exercise?

This hat is made out of natural materials.

How neatly did you copy these sentences?

Week 5 — Day 4

Here are some facts about supercomputers.
Copy each line underneath.

Supercomputers are much faster

than regular computers and have much bigger

memories. They are used to do complicated

calculations, for things like weather forecasting

and code-breaking. The world's most powerful

supercomputer is the size of two basketball courts.

How is this page looking?

Week 5 — Day 5

Here's some information about the life of Ada Lovelace. Copy it out in the space underneath.

Ada Lovelace is known for being the first computer programmer. From childhood, she was a brilliant mathematician. In the 1840s, she wrote an early version of a computer program. The program was for a machine designed by Charles Babbage for doing calculations.

How neatly did you copy this paragraph?

Week 6 — Day 1

When you add 'ation' to a verb, it turns it into a noun. Sometimes the end of the verb changes when adding 'ation'. Copy the verbs on the left once. Then copy the nouns on the right once.

inform	information
locate	location
relax	relaxation
educate	education
isolate	isolation
expect	expectation
create	creation
animate	animation
admire	admiration
meditate	meditation
organise	organisation
decorate	decoration

How was your writing on this page?

Week 6 — Day 2

These sentences all contain a noun ending in the suffix 'ation'. Copy each sentence in your neatest handwriting.

Would you like to see my new creation?

Evan and Ali had a big celebration after school.

We have given a donation to charity.

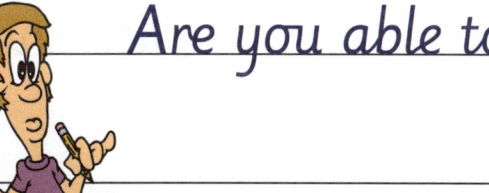

Here is your invitation to my birthday party.

Paul made a reservation at the new restaurant.

Are you able to perform this calculation?

How did you find these sentences?

Week 6 — Day 3

Here are six sentences for you to copy out. Use the lines underneath.

My younger sister is learning to ride her bicycle.

I've decided to build a sandcastle.

There will probably be fresh fruit at the market.

She wrote Jai's address on the envelope.

Riley carefully measured the length of the island.

My uncle often wins when we play chess.

How did you do on this page?

Week 6 — Day 4

This page is all about Australia.
Copy each fact out in the space below.

Australia is the sixth largest country in the world.

The Sydney Opera House is a famous landmark.

Most people live on the coast. In the middle of the country is a big desert called the 'outback'.

Wild kangaroos are unique to Australia.

Australia has more sheep than people.

How neatly did you write these facts?

Week 6 — Day 5

This paragraph is about a type of animal called a platypus. Copy it out as neatly as you can.

A platypus is a mammal from Australia. It is a strange type of mammal because it lays eggs. It also has webbed feet and a bill like a duck. A male platypus can even produce venom from its feet. A platypus swims in the water to hunt for food, and its fur is waterproof.

How did this page go?

Week 7 — Day 1

These words all end with 'que' or 'gue'. Copy each word out three times.

argue

tongue

rogue

opaque

catalogue

antique

grotesque

plague

synagogue

league

unique

colleague

How picturesque does your handwriting look?

Week 7 — Day 2

Have a go at copying out each of these sentences. They all use words containing 'que' or 'gue'.

To make a meringue, whisk egg whites with sugar.

This antique jewellery box is very valuable.

The answer is on the tip of my tongue.

I'm intrigued by your unique style.

Blue plaques mark some historical buildings.

A mosque is a place of worship for Muslims.

How neatly did you copy these sentences?

Week 7 — Day 3

Copy out each of these sentences underneath.

The vet measured the dog's height and weight.

You appear to have caught my cold.

"I'll be back in twenty minutes," I promised.

It's difficult to knit and dance at the same time.

Actually, I've realised I'm busy on Friday.

She's a popular woman, despite her singing.

How did this page go?

Week 7 — Day 4

Here is a description of a special event. Copy each line out underneath. Be as neat as you can.

When I was seven, the Queen visited my

school. I was chosen by the headteacher to greet

her, so I had to learn how to curtsey. Everyone

was really excited, but we had to be on our best

behaviour. When she arrived in her fancy car, I

felt nervous, but she smiled and asked me my name.

How does your page look?

Week 7 — Day 5

In the space below, copy out this description of a frightening forest.

The branches creaked eerily in the wind. Although there was a full moon that night, barely any light passed through the dense canopy overhead. In the pitch black, it was hard to tell whether the sounds of rustling were made by harmless forest creatures, or something else...

How did you get on with this paragraph?

Week 8 — Day 1

Copy each of these 'sc' words out three times.

scene

scenic

scientist

scientific

sceptre

muscle

discipline

ascend

descending

descendant

susceptible

adolescent

How are your 'sc' words looking?

Week 8 — Day 2

Each of these sentences has a 'sc' word in it.
Copy each sentence out below.

Tonight, there will be a crescent moon.

My sister is really good at maths and science.

I love the scent of a garden full of roses.

The climber began his ascent of the mountain.

The balloon started to descend back to Earth.

Please be very careful with those scissors.

How did you get on with these sentences?

Week 8 — Day 3

Carefully copy out these sentences on the lines below.

When you arrive, continue straight through the gate.

Be careful not to wake the sleeping guard.

Take a deep breath in, then breathe out slowly.

The top secret experiment was extremely important.

I would never have believed it was possible.

It's better to keep the fish in separate tanks.

How did you find these sentences?

Week 8 — Day 4

Here are some tips on how to be environmentally friendly. Copy them out on the lines below.

Reuse and recycle wherever you can.

Store rainwater to water plants with in dry weather.

Save kitchen scraps for the compost bin.

Switch the lights off when you leave a room.

When you grow out of your old clothes,

give them to someone else to wear.

How did you get on with these tips?

Week 8 — Day 5

This science experiment shows that water travels up a plant's stem. Copy it out in the space below.

1. Take a stick of celery with leaves on the end.

2. Add some food colouring to a glass of water.

3. Put the bottom of the celery stick in the water.

4. Leave the celery overnight.

5. The next morning, you should see that the leaves of the celery have changed colour!

How does your handwriting look today?

Week 9 — Day 1

Sometimes, 'ch' can make a 'k' sound. Here are twelve examples of words where this happens. Copy each word out twice.

chemistry

echo

ache

chaos

architect

choir

school

christening

chord

chorus

mechanic

technology

How neatly did you write these words?

Week 9 — Day 2

Copy out each of these sentences underneath.
They all have words that have a 'k' sound made by a 'ch'.

The playground at lunchtime was chaotic.

Who is your favourite character in the story?

That meal gave me a terrible stomach ache.

Chameleons can change the colour of their skin.

A sailor threw the anchor overboard.

The archaeologist uncovered a skeleton.

How do you think you did with these sentences?

Week 9 — Day 3

Copy out each of the sentences below.

The group of people smiled at me.

A strange sound was coming from the kitchen.

They've increased the price of chips!

Have you noticed anything out of the ordinary?

I believe the campsite is just straight up this road.

I think you need to try on a different size.

How did you get on with these sentences?

Week 9 — Day 4

Here are things that some children hope for when they grow up. Copy each line out underneath.

I want to live in a big house with its own pool.

I'd like to move to a hot country, such as Brazil.

I hope to be a famous tennis player.

I think I'd enjoy being a primary school teacher.

I want to own lots of snakes and lizards.

I hope to write a musical and win awards.

How do you think this page went?

Week 9 — Day 5

Here is a formal letter written to a local council. Copy it out in the space below, and add your name to the last line.

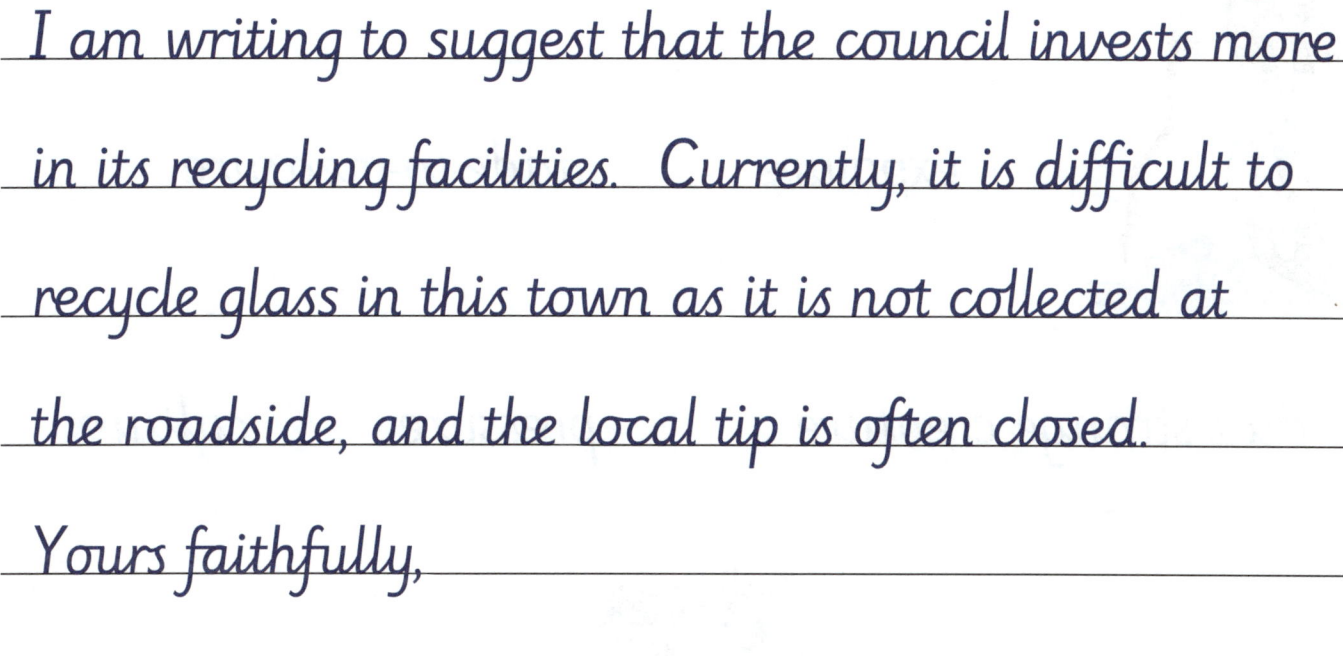

Dear Sir/Madam,

I am writing to suggest that the council invests more in its recycling facilities. Currently, it is difficult to recycle glass in this town as it is not collected at the roadside, and the local tip is often closed.

Yours faithfully,

Did you copy this letter neatly?

Week 10 — Day 1

This page contains lots of words that end in 'sure' or 'ture'.
Copy the words and phrases out underneath.

Let's go on an adventure! mixture

exposure made-to-measure

that strange creature pressure culture

temperature He is so immature.

paint a picture the football fixture

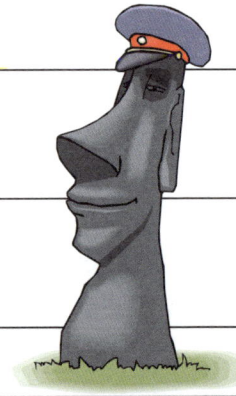

future a beautiful sculpture

How neatly did you copy this page?

Week 10 — Day 2

Copy each of these sentences out as neatly as you can.
See if you can find the words ending in 'sure' or 'ture'.

Please can you take a picture of us?

His porridge was just the right temperature.

They went for an adventure through the desert.

All of the furniture was too small for the rhino.

In the future, I want to be a nurse.

Her team were under a lot of pressure to win.

How did you get on with these sentences?

Week 10 — Day 3

Here are six sentences for you to copy out below.

King Henry the Sixth reigned in the fifteenth century.

"I promise to tidy my bedroom tonight," said Lucy.

The magician made us all disappear.

We woke up really early to get to the airport.

Finn is looking forward to the flight.

Olivia tried to describe her drawing to her aunty.

How did you find this page?

Week 10 — Day 4

This poem is about Tina's favourite things to do. Copy it out as neatly as you can.

I love flying my new kite on a sunny day,
Practising my part for the next school play,
Baking chocolate cookies with Uncle Jake,
Laughing with my friends and sitting by the lake,
Making secret dens out of sticks in the wood,
And staying in the park much longer than I should.

How neatly did you write this poem?

Week 10 — Day 5

Mia has written a thank you letter to her music teacher. Copy her letter out underneath.

Dear Mr Field,

Thank you for teaching me to play the guitar. I really enjoyed my lessons with you. You were a very helpful music teacher. I hope that you can come and watch me when I perform in the concert next week. From, Mia

How do you think this page went?

Week 11 — Day 1

Adverbs are words that describe verbs, adjectives or other adverbs. Copy these adverbs three times.

quite

very

late

perhaps

next

fast

still

already

never

often

sometimes

everywhere

How neat are your adverbs looking?

Week 11 — Day 2

Copy out each of the sentences below. They all contain at least one adverb.

I can't wait to find out what happens next.

I arrived late for my X-ray because of the snow.

She was getting quite tired of the same old jokes.

Rufus is one very talented dog!

Are you still taking flute lessons?

Our babysitter often plays board games with us.

How did you get on with these sentences?

Week 11 — Day 3

 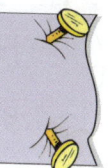

Copy out each of these sentences on the line underneath.

My calendar shows a different tractor each month.

We've had extremely dry weather recently.

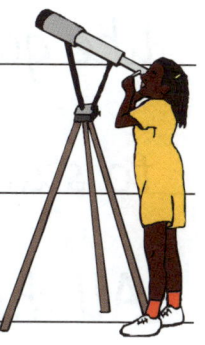

I'm particularly interested in stargazing.

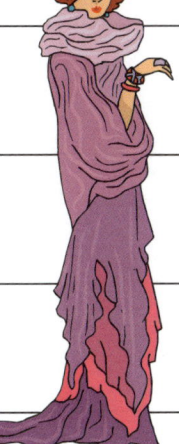

I only wear jewellery on special occasions.

There's a tartan shop in the town centre.

Mum and Dad are experienced line dancers.

How do your sentences look?

Week 11 — Day 4

Here is a postcard that Santa has written to tell the elves about his summer holiday. Copy it out below.

Christmas was hard work, so it's been great to get away for a holiday. I've been trying out lots of activities that I don't get to do at the North Pole, like golf, surfing and horse riding. I'll be back soon to start preparing for next Christmas!

All the best, Santa

How does this page look?

Week 11 — Day 5

This is part of a restaurant review. Copy it out in the space below.

I highly recommend the Topsy-Turvy Tavern. It's a unique dining experience. The menu is full of unusual dishes. I had delicious berry and vinegar ice cream for a starter, a very cheesy chocolate and olive pizza for the main course, and a really spicy gooseberry jelly for dessert.

How neatly did you copy this review?

Week 12 — Day 1

Here are some words you can use instead of 'happy'. Copy each one out three times.

pleased

glad

gleeful

merry

thrilled

cheerful

joyous

elated

beaming

delighted

overjoyed

ecstatic

Are you over the moon with your page?

Week 12 — Day 2

Copy out each of these sentences on the line below.

Books are a good source of knowledge.

You broke the cup, therefore you must pay for it.

It took a lot of strength to lift the rocket.

Out of the window, the astronaut could see Earth.

Imagine being able to eat all the sweets you want!

The queen considered herself a great dancer.

How did you get on with this page?

Week 12 — Day 3

Here are some fascinating facts about minibeasts.
Copy each one out below... if you dare!

A leafcutter ant can lift 50 times its own weight.

Spiders usually have eight eyes as well as eight legs.

Slugs have thousands of tiny teeth.

The world's longest earthworm is two metres long.

To make enough honey to fill one jar, a single bee would have to visit two million flowers.

Do your facts look fantastic?

Week 12 — Day 4

Copy out this paragraph about the Lake District as neatly as you can.

The Lake District is an area of land in North-West England. It is famous for its 16 lakes, as well as its many hills and forests. Over 15 million people visit every year. It's a popular place to go walking, biking, kayaking, and more. If you visit, you might spot a red squirrel, or maybe even a golden eagle!

___

___

___

___

___

How did you get on with the paragraph?

Week 12 — Day 5

Here is the first verse of the poem, 'In Summer'. Copy it out on the lines below.

In Summer, by Paul Laurence Dunbar

Oh, summer has clothed the earth

In a cloak from the loom of the sun!

And a mantle, too, of the skies' soft blue,

And a belt where the rivers run.

How does your copy of this verse look?